outdoor
eating

Easy dishes to cook at home

This edition published in 2010
LOVE FOOD is an imprint of Parragon Books Ltd

Parragon
Queen Street House
4 Queen Street
Bath BA1 1HE, UK

ISBN: 978-1-4075-8104-0

Printed in China

Designed by Talking Design
Cover and introduction text by Lorraine Turner

Notes for the Reader
This book uses imperial, metric, and US cup measurements. Follow the same units of measurement throughout; do not mix imperial and metric. All spoon measurements are level: teaspoons are assumed to be 5 ml, and tablespoons are assumed to be 15 ml. Unless otherwise stated, milk is assumed to be whole, eggs and individual vegetables such as potatoes are medium, and pepper is freshly ground black pepper.

The times given are an approximate guide only. Preparation times differ according to the techniques used by different people and the cooking times may also vary from those given as a result of the type of oven used. Optional ingredients, variations or serving suggestions have not been included in the calculations.

Recipes using raw or very lightly cooked eggs should be avoided by infants, the elderly, pregnant women, convalescents, and anyone with a chronic condition. Pregnant and breastfeeding women are advised to avoid eating peanuts and peanut products. Sufferers from nut allergies should be aware that some of the ready-prepared ingredients used in the recipes in this book may contain nuts. Always check the packaging before use.

Contents

introduction

What could be better for a successful social occasion than gathering a group of friends and loved ones in the open air for some delicious outdoor dining? This is the stuff of cherished memories!

Balmy summer days spent basking in the warmth of the sun, lots of entertaining conversation and lively company, all based around the wonderful intimacy of a communal meal. People have been eating outdoors since ancient times, from nomadic tribes eating on the move, to indigenous people wanting simply to enjoy the many benefits of clean fresh air, and friendly company. In warmer climates, such as in the Mediterranean, dining outside is a tradition, where all members of the household gather round a table in the garden or on the terrace and spend some lively hours eating, drinking, and talking together. Yet it is also possible for people in cooler climates to enjoy this great custom, and more and more people are discovering the joys of eating outdoor meals together.

One of the great benefits of outdoor eating is its versatility. For example, you could pack a tempting selection of cold foods and drinks into cooler bags, hampers, or rucksacks for the

perfect portable meal. Simply find a comfortable spot with a scenic view and the scene is set for a very memorable feast. If you want to be more ambitious, there is nothing like cooking in the fresh air to instill a sense of excitement and anticipation. Who can resist the mouthwatering smell and sound of juicy cuts of meat sizzling on a barbecue, or succulent morsels of fish, and vegetables barbecued in a tasty sauce?

Preparing and cooking outdoor meals

Preparing and cooking an outdoor meal doesn't have to be difficult. All of the recipes in this book are easy to prepare and cook—ideal if you have a busy lifestyle with not much time to spare. If you are arranging a barbecue, here are a few simple tips to ensure it is a success and help you get the most out of the occasion:

• Harmful bacteria tend to multiply in warmer weather outdoors, so wash your hands thoroughly before, and after preparing food.

• Pack some napkins so that you and your guests can clean your hands before and after eating.

• Keep all food covered with plastic wrap to protect it from flies.

• Thaw any frozen foods thoroughly before cooking.

• Never reuse a marinade, especially one that has been used to marinate meat or poultry. Throw it away after use.

• Barbecued food tends to brown quickly on the outside without cooking on the inside, so ensure all meat and poultry is cooked thoroughly, all the way through, and is piping hot before serving.

If necessary, partly cook the food indoors first and then finish cooking it on the barbecue (but never do it the other way round: in other words, never partly cook it on the barbecue then finish it off in the kitchen later).

• Use separate utensils—such as knives, forks, chopping boards, and cooking tongs—for cooked and raw meat, and poultry to prevent cross-contamination from potentially harmful bacteria.

• Don't leave foods standing around in the open air or at the wrong temperature—keep hot foods hot, and cold foods chilled until ready to serve.

• If the weather is very hot, throw away any uneaten barbecued food that has been left out for more than two or three hours.

• Keep any children and pets away from preparation/cooking areas and utensils.

• Take extra care to position your barbecue so that the smoke will not be a nuisance to other people.

• Whether you are using a coal, hardwood, or electric barbecue, always follow the safety instructions that come with your barbecue, and take extra care when using fuel and naked flames.

Follow these simple tips and you will have all the ingredients you need for a safe and enjoyable alfresco meal. All that remains is for you to have fun and enjoy yourself!

the salad
bowl

Traditional
Greek Salad

SERVES 4

7 oz/200 g Greek feta cheese

½ head of iceberg lettuce or 1 lettuce
such as romaine or escarole,
shredded or sliced

4 tomatoes, quartered

½ cucumber, sliced

12 Greek black olives, stoned

2 tbsp chopped fresh herbs such as
oregano, flat-leaf parsley, mint or
basil

Dressing

6 tbsp extra virgin olive oil

2 tbsp fresh lemon juice

1 garlic clove, crushed

pinch of sugar

salt and pepper

Make the dressing by whisking the ingredients together in a small bowl. Set aside. Cut the cheese into cubes about 1 inch/2.5 cm square. Put the lettuce, tomatoes, and cucumber in a salad bowl. Scatter over the cheese and toss together.

Just before serving, whisk the dressing, pour over the salad leaves and toss together. Scatter over the olives and chopped herbs and serve.

Three-Color
Salad

SERVES 4

10 oz/280 g buffalo mozzarella,
  drained and thinly sliced

8 plum tomatoes, sliced

20 fresh basil leaves

½ cup extra virgin olive oil

salt and pepper

Arrange the mozzarella and tomato slices on 4 individual serving plates and season to taste with salt. Set aside in a cool place for 30 minutes.

Sprinkle the basil leaves over the salad and drizzle with the olive oil. Season with pepper and serve immediately.

Seafood & Spinach
Salad

SERVES 4

1 lb 2 oz/500 g live mussels, soaked
   and cleaned

3¹/₂ oz/100 g shrimp, peeled and
   deveined

12 oz/350 g scallops

1 lb 2 oz/500 g baby spinach leaves

3 scallions, trimmed and sliced

Dressing

4 tbsp extra virgin olive oil

2 tbsp white wine vinegar

1 tbsp lemon juice

1 tsp lemon zest, finely grated

1 garlic clove, chopped

1 tbsp fresh ginger, grated

1 small red chile, seeded and diced

1 tbsp chopped fresh cilantro

salt and pepper

Put the mussels into a large pan with a little water, bring to a boil, and cook over high heat for 4 minutes. Drain and reserve the liquid. Discard any mussels that remain closed. Return the reserved liquid to the pan and bring to a boil. Add the shrimp and scallops and cook for 3 minutes. Drain. Remove the mussels from their shells. Rinse the mussels, shrimp, and scallops in cold water, drain, and put them in a large bowl. Cool, cover with plastic wrap, and chill for 45 minutes. Meanwhile, rinse the baby spinach leaves and transfer them to a pan with 4 tablespoons of water. Cook over high heat for 1 minute, transfer to a strainer, refresh under cold running water, and drain.

To make the dressing, put all the ingredients into a small bowl and mix. Arrange the spinach on serving dishes, then scatter over half of the scallions. Top with the mussels, shrimp, and scallops, then scatter over the remaining scallions. Drizzle over the dressing and serve.

Warm
Pasta Salad

SERVES 4

8 oz/225 g dried farfalle or
   other pasta shapes

6 pieces of sun-dried tomato in oil,
   drained and chopped

4 scallions, chopped

1¼ cups arugula, shredded

½ cucumber, seeded and diced

salt and pepper

Dressing

4 tbsp olive oil

1 tbsp white wine vinegar

½ tsp superfine sugar

1 tsp Dijon mustard

salt and pepper

4 fresh basil leaves, finely shredded

To make the dressing, whisk the olive oil, vinegar, sugar, and mustard together in a bowl or pitcher. Season to taste with salt and pepper and stir in the basil.

Bring a large heavy-bottom pan of lightly salted water to a boil. Add the pasta, return to a boil, and cook for 8–10 minutes, or until tender but still firm to the bite. Drain and transfer to a salad bowl. Add the dressing and toss well.

Add the tomatoes, scallions, arugula, and cucumber, season to taste with salt and pepper, and toss. Serve warm.

Warm Red Lentil Salad
with Goat Cheese

SERVES 4

2 tbsp olive oil

2 tsp cumin seeds

2 garlic cloves, crushed

2 tsp fresh ginger, grated

1½ cups split red lentils

3 cups vegetable stock

2 tbsp fresh mint, chopped

2 tbsp fresh cilantro, chopped

2 red onions, thinly sliced

4½ cups baby spinach leaves

1 tsp hazelnut oil

5½ oz/150 g soft goat cheese

4 tbsp plain yogurt, strained

pepper

Heat half the olive oil in a large pan over medium heat, add the cumin seeds, garlic, and ginger and cook for 2 minutes, stirring constantly.

Stir in the lentils, then add the stock, a ladleful at a time, until it is all absorbed, stirring constantly—this will take about 20 minutes. Remove from the heat and stir in the herbs.

Meanwhile, heat the remaining olive oil in a skillet over medium heat, add the onions, and cook, stirring frequently, for 10 minutes, or until soft and lightly browned.

Toss the spinach in the hazelnut oil in a bowl, then divide among 4 serving plates.

Mash the goat cheese with the yogurt in a small bowl and season to taste with pepper.

Divide the lentils among the serving plates and top with the onions and goat cheese mixture.

Raspberry & Feta Salad
with Couscous

SERVES 4

12 oz/350 g couscous

2½ cups boiling chicken stock or
   vegetable stock

12 oz/350 g fresh raspberries

small bunch of fresh basil

8 oz/225 g feta cheese, cubed or
   crumbled

2 zucchini, thinly sliced

4 scallions, trimmed and diagonally
   sliced

⅓ cup pine nuts, toasted

1 lemon rind, grated

Dressing

1 tbsp white wine vinegar

1 tbsp balsamic vinegar

4 tbsp extra virgin olive oil

juice of 1 lemon

salt and pepper

Put the couscous in a large heatproof bowl and pour over the stock. Stir well, then cover and let soak until all the stock has been absorbed.

Pick over the raspberries, discarding any that are overripe. Shred the basil leaves.

Transfer the couscous to a large serving bowl and stir well to break up any lumps. Add the cheese, zucchini, scallions, raspberries, and pine nuts. Stir in the basil and lemon rind and gently toss all the ingredients together.

Put all the dressing ingredients in a screw-top jar, with salt and pepper to taste, then screw on the lid and shake until well blended. Pour over the salad and serve.

Caesar
Salad

SERVES 4

²/₃ cup olive oil

2 garlic cloves

5 slices white bread, crusts removed,
   cut into ½-inch/1-cm cubes

1 large egg

2 romaine lettuces or 3 Boston
   lettuces

2 tbsp lemon juice

salt and pepper

8 canned anchovy fillets, drained and
   coarsely chopped

³/₄ cup fresh Parmesan cheese
   shavings

Bring a small, heavy-bottom pan of water to a boil.

Meanwhile, heat 4 tablespoons of the olive oil in a heavy-bottom skillet. Add the garlic and cubed bread and cook, stirring and tossing frequently, for 4–5 minutes, or until the bread is crispy and golden all over. Remove from the skillet with a slotted spoon and drain on paper towels.

Add the egg to the boiling water and cook for 1 minute, then remove from the pan and set aside.

Arrange the salad greens in a salad bowl. Mix the remaining olive oil and lemon juice together, then season to taste with salt and pepper. Crack the egg into the dressing and whisk to blend. Pour the dressing over the salad greens, toss well, then add the croutons and chopped anchovies and toss the salad again. Sprinkle with Parmesan cheese shavings and serve.

the
grill

Boozy Beef
Steaks

SERVES 4

4 beef steaks

4 tbsp whiskey or brandy

2 tbsp soy sauce

1 tbsp dark brown sugar

tomato slices

pepper

fresh parsley sprigs, to garnish

garlic bread, to serve

Make a few cuts in the edge of the fat on each steak. This will stop the meat curling as it cooks. Place the meat in a shallow, nonmetallic dish.

Mix the whiskey, soy sauce, sugar, and pepper to taste together in a small bowl, stirring until the sugar dissolves. Pour the mixture over the steak. Cover with plastic wrap and let marinate in the refrigerator for at least 2 hours.

Preheat the barbecue. Cook the beef steaks over hot coals, searing the meat over the hottest part of the grill for 2 minutes on each side.

Move the meat to an area with slightly less intense heat and cook for an additional 4–10 minutes on each side, depending on how well done you like your steaks. To test if the meat is cooked, insert the point of a sharp knife into the meat—the juices will run from red when the meat is still rare, to clear as it becomes well cooked.

Lightly grill the tomato slices for 1–2 minutes. Transfer the meat and the tomatoes to warmed serving plates. Garnish with fresh parsley sprigs and serve with garlic bread.

Surf 'n' Turf
Skewers

SERVES 2

8 oz/225 g beef tenderloin, about
   1-inch/2.5-cm thick

8 raw jumbo shrimp, in their shells

4 tbsp butter

2 garlic cloves, crushed

3 tbsp chopped fresh parsley, plus
   extra parsley sprigs, to garnish

finely grated rind and juice of 1 lime

salt and pepper

lime wedges, to garnish

crusty bread, to serve

Cut the steak into 1-inch/2.5-cm cubes. To prepare the shrimp, pull off their heads with your fingers, then peel off their shells, leaving the tails on. Using a sharp knife, make a shallow slit along the back of each shrimp, then pull out the dark vein and discard. Rinse the shrimp under cold running water and dry well on paper towels.

Alternating them, thread an equal number of the steak cubes and shrimp onto 2 oiled metal kebab skewers or presoaked wooden skewers. Season the kebab to taste with pepper.

Preheat the barbecue. Meanwhile, put the butter and garlic into a small pan and heat gently until melted. Remove from the heat and add the parsley, lime rind and juice, and salt and pepper to taste. Leave in a warm place so that the butter remains melted.

Brush the kebab with a little of the melted butter. Put the kebab onto an oiled rack and cook over medium heat for 4–8 minutes until the steak is cooked according to your taste and the shrimp turn pink, turning the kebab frequently during cooking, and brushing with the remaining melted butter.

Serve the kebab hot on the skewers, with the remaining butter spooned over. Garnish with lime wedges and parsley sprigs and serve with crusty bread to mop up the buttery juices.

Pork Sausages
with Thyme

SERVES 4

1 garlic clove, finely chopped

1 onion, grated

1 small red chile, seeded and finely chopped

1 lb/450 g lean ground pork

scant ⅔ cup almonds, toasted and ground

1 cup fresh breadcrumbs

1 tbsp finely chopped fresh thyme

salt and pepper

flour, for dusting

vegetable oil, for brushing

To Serve

fresh hotdog rolls

slices of onion, lightly cooked

ketchup and or mustard

Put the garlic, onion, chile, pork, almonds, breadcrumbs, and thyme into a large bowl. Season well with salt and pepper and mix until well combined.

Using your hands, form the mixture into sausage shapes. Roll each sausage in a little flour, then transfer to a bowl, cover with plastic wrap, and let chill for 45 minutes.

Preheat the barbecue. Brush a piece of foil with oil, then put the sausages on the foil and brush them with a little more vegetable oil. Transfer the sausages, still in the foil, to the barbecue.

Barbecue over hot coals, turning the sausages frequently, for about 15 minutes, or until cooked through. Serve with hotdog rolls, cooked sliced onion, and ketchup.

Jerk
Chicken

SERVES 4

4 lean chicken pieces

1 bunch of scallions, trimmed

1–2 chiles (Scotch bonnet, if possible)

1 garlic clove

2-inch/5-cm piece of fresh ginger,
  peeled and roughly chopped

1/2 tsp dried thyme

1/2 tsp paprika

1/4 tsp ground allspice

pinch ground cinnamon

pinch ground cloves

4 tbsp white wine vinegar

3 tbsp light soy sauce

pepper

Rinse the chicken pieces and pat them dry on paper towels. Place them in a shallow dish.

Place the scallions, chiles, garlic, ginger, thyme, paprika, allspice, cinnamon, cloves, wine vinegar, soy sauce, and pepper to taste in a food processor and process until smooth.

Pour the spicy mixture over the chicken. Turn the chicken pieces over so that they are well coated in the marinade.

Transfer the chicken parts to the refrigerator and leave to marinate for up to 24 hours.

Remove the chicken from the marinade and grill over medium hot coals for about 30 minutes, turning the chicken over and basting occasionally with any remaining marinade, until the chicken is browned and cooked through.

Transfer the chicken pieces to individual serving plates and serve at once.

Coconut
Shrimp

SERVES 4

6 scallions

1³/₄ cups coconut milk

finely grated rind and juice of 1 lime

4 tbsp chopped fresh cilantro, plus
    extra to garnish

2 tbsp corn oil

pepper

1 lb 7 oz/650 g raw jumbo shrimp,
    deveined

lemon wedges, to garnish

Finely chop the scallions and place in a large, shallow, nonmetallic dish with the coconut milk, lime rind and juice, cilantro, and oil. Mix well and season to taste with pepper. Add the shrimp, turning to coat. Cover with plastic wrap and let marinate in the refrigerator for 1 hour.

Preheat the barbecue. Drain the shrimp, reserving the marinade. Thread the shrimp onto 8 long metal skewers.

Cook the skewers over medium hot coals, brushing with the reserved marinade and turning frequently, for 8 minutes, or until they have changed color. Serve the shrimp immediately, garnished with the lemon wedges and chopped cilantro.

Greek Vegetable
Kebabs

SERVES 4

2 onions

8 new potatoes, washed but not
  peeled

salt

1 eggplant, cut into 8 pieces

8 thick slices cucumber

1 red bell pepper, seeded and cut into
  8 pieces

1 yellow bell pepper, seeded and cut
  into 8 pieces

8 oz/225 g provolone cheese, cut into
  8 cubes

2 nectarines, pitted and cut into
  wedges

8 button mushrooms

2 tbsp olive oil

2 tsp chopped fresh thyme

2 tsp chopped fresh rosemary

cucumber and yogurt dip, to serve

Preheat the barbecue. Cut the onions into wedges, then place the onions and potatoes in a pan of lightly salted boiling water and cook for 20 minutes, or until just tender. Drain and let cool. Meanwhile, blanch the eggplant in boiling water for 2 minutes, then add the cucumber and let simmer for 1 minute. Add the bell peppers and let simmer for 2 minutes, then drain and let the vegetables cool.

Place the cooled vegetables, cheese, nectarines, and mushrooms in a bowl. Add the olive oil and herbs and toss to coat. Thread the vegetables, cheese, nectarines, and mushrooms onto several metal skewers.

Cook the kebabs over hot coals, turning frequently, for 15 minutes. Transfer to a large serving plate and serve immediately with the cucumber and yogurt dip.

the
plate

Ciabatta
Sandwiches

MAKES 4

2 loaves ciabatta bread

extra virgin olive oil

about 8 oz/225 g cherry tomatoes,
   halved

8 thin slices prosciutto

1 small bunch fresh basil leaves

salt and pepper

Using a serrated knife, cut each loaf of bread in half through the center horizontally, then brush the cut sides with olive oil. Sprinkle the bottom halves with salt and pepper to taste, then divide the tomato halves among the bottom pieces of bread, cut sides down.

Top each sandwich base with 2 slices of prosciutto, folded to fit as necessary, then add fresh basil leaves. Place the tops on the sandwiches and press down, crushing the tomatoes into the bread.

Preheat a sandwich toaster or griddle and brush the bread with a little oil. Toast the sandwiches lightly, to brown and crisp the crust, turning them once if cooking on a griddle. Serve immediately.

Mixed Vegetable
Bruschetta

SERVES 4

olive oil, for brushing and drizzling

1 red bell pepper, halved and seeded

1 orange bell pepper, halved and
   seeded

4 thick slices baguette or ciabatta

1 fennel bulb, sliced

1 red onion, sliced

2 zucchini, diagonally sliced

2 garlic cloves, halved

1 tomato, halved

salt and pepper

fresh sage leaves, to garnish

Brush the barbecue rack with oil and heat the coals. Cut each bell pepper in half lengthwise into 4 strips. Toast the bread on both sides in a toaster or under a broiler.

When the barbecue is hot add the bell peppers and fennel and cook for 4 minutes, then add the onion and zucchini, and cook for 5 minutes, until all the vegetables are tender but still with a slight "bite." If necessary, cook the vegetables in 2 batches, as they should be placed on the barbecue in a single layer.

Meanwhile, rub the garlic halves over the toasts, then rub them with the tomato halves. Place on warm plates. Pile the chargrilled vegetables on top of the toasts, drizzle with olive oil, and season with salt and pepper. Garnish with sage leaves and serve warm.

Panzanella

SERVES 4–6

9 oz/250 g stale focaccia, ciabatta,
   or French bread
4 large, vine-ripened tomatoes
about 6 tbsp extra virgin olive oil
4 red, yellow, and/or orange bell
   peppers
3½ oz/100 g cucumber
1 large red onion, finely chopped
8 canned anchovy fillets, drained and
   chopped
2 tbsp capers in brine, rinsed and
   patted dry
about 4 tbsp red wine vinegar
about 2 tbsp balsamic vinegar
salt and pepper
fresh basil leaves, to garnish

Cut the bread into 1-inch/2.5-cm cubes and place in a large bowl. Working over a plate to catch any juices, quarter the tomatoes; reserve the juices. Using a teaspoon, scoop out the cores and seeds and discard, then finely chop the flesh. Add to the bread cubes. Drizzle 5 tablespoons of the oil over the mixture and toss with your hands until well coated. Pour in the reserved tomato juice and toss again. Set aside for about 30 minutes.

Meanwhile, cut the bell peppers in half and remove the cores and seeds. Place on a metal rack under a preheated hot broiler and broil for 10 minutes, or until the skins are charred and the flesh soft. Place in a plastic bag, seal, and set aside for 20 minutes to allow the steam to loosen the skins. Remove the skins, then finely chop. Cut the cucumber in half lengthwise, then cut each half into 3 strips lengthwise. Using a teaspoon, scoop out and discard the seeds. Dice the cucumber.

Add the onion, peppers, cucumber, anchovy fillets, and capers to the bread and toss together. Sprinkle with the red wine vinegar and balsamic vinegar and season to taste with salt and pepper. Drizzle with extra olive oil or vinegar if necessary, but take care that it does not become too greasy or soggy. Sprinkle the fresh basil leaves over the salad and serve at once.

Tabbouleh

SERVES 4

1 cup bulgur wheat

3 tbsp extra virgin olive oil

4 tbsp lemon juice

4 scallions

1 green bell pepper, seeded and sliced

4 tomatoes, chopped

2 tbsp chopped fresh parsley

2 tbsp chopped fresh mint

8 black olives, pitted

salt and pepper

fresh mint sprigs, to garnish

Place the bulgur wheat in a large bowl and add enough cold water to cover. Let stand for 30 minutes, or until the wheat has doubled in size. Drain well and press out as much liquid as possible. Spread out the wheat on paper towels to dry.

Place the wheat in a serving bowl. Mix the olive oil and lemon juice together in a measuring cup and season to taste with salt and pepper. Pour the lemon mixture over the wheat and let marinate for 1 hour.

Using a sharp knife, finely chop the scallions, then add to the salad with the green bell pepper, tomatoes, parsley, and mint, and toss lightly to mix. Top the salad with the olives and garnish with fresh mint sprigs, then serve.

Stuffed
Grape Leaves

MAKES ABOUT 30

8 oz/225 g package grape leaves
    preserved in brine

¾ cup olive oil

1 small onion, finely chopped

1 garlic clove, finely chopped

generous ½ cup short-grain rice,
    cooked and cooled

⅓ cup pine nuts, chopped

⅓ cup currants

3 scallions, finely chopped

1 tbsp chopped fresh mint

1 tbsp chopped fresh dill

2 tbsp chopped fresh flat-leaf parsley

juice of 1 lemon

¼ pint/50 ml water

salt and pepper

lemon wedges, to serve

Place the grape leaves in a large bowl, pour over boiling water, and leave to soak for 20 minutes. Drain, soak in cold water for 20 minutes, and then drain again. Heat 2 tablespoons of the oil in a large, heavy-bottomed skillet, add the onion and garlic, and cook for 5–10 minutes until softened. Add the onions to the cooked rice with the pine nuts, currants, scallions, mint, dill, and parsley. Season with a little salt and plenty of pepper and mix the ingredients well together.

Place 1 grape leaf, vein-side upward, on a work surface. Put a little filling on the base of the leaf and fold up the bottom ends of the leaf. Fold the sides of the leaf into the center then roll up the leaf around the filling. Squeeze the packet gently in your hand to seal. Continue filling and rolling the grape leaves until all the ingredients have been used up, putting any torn grape leaves in the bottom of a large flameproof casserole or Dutch oven. Put the stuffed leaves, seam-side down and in a single layer, in the casserole, packing them as close together as possible.

Mix the remaining oil and the lemon juice with ⅔ cup water and pour into the casserole. Place a large plate over the grape leaves to keep them in place, then cover the casserole with a lid. Bring to a simmer and simmer for 45 minutes. Leave the grape leaves to cool in the liquid. Serve the grape leaves warm or chilled, with lemon wedges.

Coleslaw

SERVES 10–12

⅔ cup mayonnaise

⅔ cup plain yogurt

dash of Tabasco sauce

1 medium head of white cabbage

4 carrots

1 green bell pepper

salt and pepper

To make the dressing, mix the mayonnaise, yogurt, Tabasco sauce, and salt and pepper to taste together in a small bowl. Chill in the refrigerator until required.

Cut the cabbage in half and then into quarters. Remove and discard the tough center stem and finely shred the leaves. Wash the leaves under cold running water and dry thoroughly on paper towels. Peel the carrots and shred in a food processor or on a mandoline. Alternatively, roughly grate the carrot. Cut the bell pepper into quarters, then seed it and cut the flesh into thin strips.

Mix the vegetables together in a large serving bowl and toss to mix. Pour over the dressing and toss until the vegetables are well coated. Let the vegetable mixture chill until required.

the
glass

Fresh
Lemonade

MAKES 1.2 PINTS/1.2 LITERS

4 large lemons, preferably unwaxed
 or organic

3/4 cup superfine sugar

3 1/2 cups boiling water

ice cubes, to serve

Scrub the lemons well, then dry. Using a vegetable peeler, peel 3 of the lemons very thinly. Place the peel in a large pitcher or bowl, add the sugar and boiling water and stir well until the sugar has dissolved. Cover the jug and leave to stand for at least 3 hours, stirring occasionally. Meanwhile, squeeze the juice from the 3 lemons and reserve.

Strain the lemon peel and stir in the reserved lemon juice. Thinly slice the remaining lemon and cut the slices in half. Add to the lemonade together with the ice cubes. Stir and serve.

Orange & Lime
Iced Tea

SERVES 2

1¼ cups water

2 tea bags

scant ½ cup orange juice

4 tbsp lime juice

1–2 tbsp brown sugar

8 ice cubes

To Decorate

wedge of lime

granulated sugar

slices of fresh orange, lemon, or lime

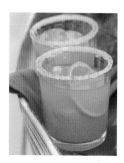

Pour the water into a pan and bring to a boil. Remove from the heat, add the tea bags, and let stand for 5 minutes to infuse.

Remove the tea bags and let the tea cool to room temperature (about 30 minutes). Transfer to a pitcher, cover with plastic wrap, and chill in the refrigerator for at least 45 minutes.

When the tea has chilled, pour in the orange juice and lime juice. Add sugar to taste.

Take two glasses and rub the rims with a wedge of lime, then dip them in granulated sugar to frost. Put the ice cubes into the glasses and pour over the tea. Decorate with slices of fresh orange, lemon, or lime and serve.

Raspberry
Crush

SERVES 4

10½ oz/300 g fresh or thawed frozen
 raspberries

4 tbsp orange juice

1–2 tsp clear honey, or to taste

crushed ice

1¼ cups soda water

4 scoops raspberry sorbet
 or frozen raspberry yogurt

Reserve a few raspberries for the decoration then put the remainder in a smoothie machine or blender. Switch on and, with the motor running, add the orange juice and blend for 1 minute.

Add the honey to taste and blend for 20 seconds. Half-fill a tumbler with the crushed ice and top up with the soda water. Place a scoop of raspberry sorbet on top and serve decorated with the reserved raspberries.

Singapore
Sling

SERVES 1

10–12 cracked ice cubes

2 measures gin

1 measure cherry brandy

1 measure lemon juice

1 tsp grenadine

soda water, to top off

lime peel and cocktail cherries,
   to decorate

Put 4–6 cracked ice cubes into a cocktail shaker. Pour the gin, cherry brandy, lemon juice, and grenadine over the ice. Shake vigorously until a frost forms.

Half fill a chilled highball glass with cracked ice cubes and strain the cocktail over them. Top off with soda water and then decorate with a twist of lime peel and cocktail cherries.

Soft
Sangria

MAKES 3¹/₂ PINTS/2 LITERS

6 cups red grape juice

1¼ cups orange juice

5 tbsp cranberry juice

4 tbsp lemon juice

4 tbsp lime juice

½ cup sugar syrup

ice cubes

slices of lemon, orange, and lime,
  to decorate

Put the grape juice, orange juice, cranberry juice, lemon juice, lime juice, and sugar syrup into a chilled punch bowl and stir well.

Add the ice and decorate with the slices of lemon, orange, and lime.

Margarita

SERVES 1

lime wedge

coarse salt

4–6 cracked ice cubes

3 measures white tequila

1 measure triple sec

2 measures lime juice

slice of lime, to decorate

Rub the rim of a chilled cocktail glass with the lime wedge and then dip in a saucer of coarse salt to frost.

Put the cracked ice cubes into a cocktail shaker. Pour the tequila, triple sec, and lime juice over the ice. Shake vigorously until a frost forms.

Strain into the prepared glass and decorate with the lime slice.